DIMINUTIVE COMEDIES
FOR WOMEN

F. SLADEN-SMITH

Diminutive Comedies
for Women

LONDON
J. GARNET MILLER LTD.
54 Victoria Street, S.W.1

THIS FIFTH IMPRESSION PUBLISHED BY
J. GARNET MILLER LTD.
IN 1961
PRINTED IN GREAT BRITAIN
BY BUTLER & TANNER LTD.
FROME & LONDON

THIS BOOK WAS FIRST PUBLISHED IN 1942 BY
FREDERICK MULLER LTD.
SECOND IMPRESSION, 1945
THIRD IMPRESSION (BY J. GARNET MILLER LTD.) 1952
FOURTH IMPRESSION, 1958

CONTENTS

NOTE : In each play all directions
from the auditorium.

To DOROTHY

AND ELSIE CROSSE

MARY CALLS THE CATTLE HOME

The SCENE *is supposed to represent a small exhibition room. There is a bench in the centre, or two chairs.*

[*The* 1ST WOMAN *enters on the right. The* 2ND WOMAN, *who has been standing near on the left, comes up to her.*

1ST WOMAN (*looking round*) : I suppose this is the exhibition ? What a queer little room.

2ND WOMAN : Yes, this is the exhibition. Good morning. I'm sorry you don't like the room. I think it's such a nice one.

1ST WOMAN : Well, I don't know how you can. Stuffy—and all those dreadful stairs. I really must sit down for a moment. (*Sits.*) And you had better come and sit beside me. I always like someone to talk to, and you must be tired of looking at these fearful pictures.

2ND WOMAN (*sitting down beside her*) : How do you know they're fearful ? You haven't seen them yet.

1ST WOMAN : Most of the papers seemed to think they were awful ; and the artist herself is a most impossible woman, I'm told.

2ND WOMAN : Oh, really ? I should hardly have said that.

1ST WOMAN : Do you know her ?

2ND WOMAN : Slightly.

1ST WOMAN : And isn't she an absolute freak ? All art and crafty, with hardly any morals . . . and dressed like a camouflaged aerodrome ? Smokes cigars, I understand, and probably takes drugs.

2ND WOMAN (*rising*) : Who told you all these disgusting and perfectly untrue things ?

1ST WOMAN : Oh, I don't know. Do sit down again ; it makes me tired to see you standing. (2ND WOMAN *sits*) As for what one hears—you can't stop people talking, can you, and, of course, the critics——

2ND WOMAN (*with scorn*) : The critics ! If artists bothered about what critics say they'd all go mad and shoot themselves.

I

1ST WOMAN (*comfortably*) : Nevertheless, they do bother, quite a lot. The pity of it is that although they bother, so few go and shoot themselves.

2ND WOMAN : You believe in the extermination of artists !

1ST WOMAN · Well, not those who have really made a *name*, of course, but the smaller fry—I mean, look at these pictures ! Did you ever see such travesties ?

2ND WOMAN (*warmly*) : I think some of the pictures here are very good, and one or two are magnificent. I'm sure of that !

1ST WOMAN : Well, your tastes must be very different from mine. I knew how bad the pictures would be, and only came because my cousin, Christabel, who is a bit of an artist—I mean she does leather-work quite prettily—said a one-woman show ought to be supported, because, despite everything, women were still not getting absolutely the best of it. But, really, they're worse than I expected. Look at them ! Mad, the whole lot. Fortunately, I can see that without stirring.

2ND WOMAN : I'm sorry, but I must disagree with you profoundly. Far from being mad, each picture has its own rhythmic values.

1ST WOMAN : Well, of course, that means nothing to me. I can only see a collection of daubs. I mean, look at this thing in front of us. All that pink and yellow rubbish. (*Leaning back and surveying the picture, which, of course, is placed on the imaginary " fourth wall."*) It seems to be rather like a modern carpet. . . I can just imagine some silly cows spattered about . . .

2ND WOMAN (*indignant*) : Oh, can you really ? Cows, indeed !

1ST WOMAN (*dreamily*) : Yes, cows, distinctly cows . . . and then vast stretches of yellow sands.

2ND WOMAN (*surprised*) : Where do you see the stretches of sand ?

1ST WOMAN : My dear, they're quite obvious ; there's sand all over the place. (*Amused*) Fancy me having to explain a modern picture to anybody. How Christabel would laugh ! Yes, cows wandering about on sand . . . and at the top there are marks certainly representing water . . . really, I'm getting quite interested in the picture, after all !

2

2ND WOMAN : So I see. (*With sarcasm*) Very good of you. Cows, sand and water. Do you happen to know what the picture is called ?

1ST WOMAN : Of course I don't. I never bother to buy a catalogue. What is it called ?

2ND WOMAN : Floral Symphony in Mauve.

1ST WOMAN : But that's just ridiculous. It's not in the least floral, and there isn't any mauve—unless that violet splotch in the corner—and, of course, it isn't a splotch, it's a girl.

2ND WOMAN (*jumping up*) : No, really, this is too much ! Where on earth can you see a girl ?

1ST WOMAN : Do sit down, your constant activity is so fidgeting. (2ND WOMAN *sits again.*) The girl's over there looking at the cows. Not badly drawn either ; she's a little like Christabel. Do you know, this picture becomes clearer to me every moment. There is the water . . . probably some river . . . and the cows and the girl. . . . Oh ! (*Jumping up in great excitement.*) I've got it ! It's Mary calling the cattle home !

2ND WOMAN (*jumping up*) : Nonsense ! This is frankly insulting !

1ST WOMAN : Don't be absurd. How can it be insulting ? I can see it all now. There is the river Dee and its sands— " Across the sands of Dee," you know the dear old poem, why, I used to recite it myself years ago—and there are the cows— really, the cows are quite lifelike—and there is Mary and the boat they will use later—you remember, " They rowed her in across the curling foam, the cruel, hungry foam,"—and, I declare, there is the foam as hungry as anything ! Really, this picture is good, definitely good. And to think I should have to explain it to you ! Too, too funny——

2ND WOMAN : Stop ! You've said enough. This is blasphemy ! Oh, the general public ! Always asking for a meaning, never happy unless a picture tells a story ! Heaven help the poor artist at the hands of the public ! Let me tell you this work is entirely psychological ; it is the inner emotions produced by a mass of leaves and flowers dimly sensed in a French forest. It is a symbolical exercise in abstract form. And all you can see are the wretched sands of Dee, with Mary and a boat and curling foam and a lot of silly cows ! You are wrong from begin-

3

ning to end, and if a picture with a story is your idea of art, why don't you stick to the Royal Academy?

1ST WOMAN : Well, really, what an outburst! Quite ill-mannered, too. You seem to know all about the picture, but you've certainly spoilt my enjoyment of it. I *was* going to buy it, but now——

2ND WOMAN : WHAT? You were going to buy it????

1ST WOMAN : Yes, I was, for Christabel. She's getting married on the fifth, but after what you have——

2ND WOMAN (*with complete change of tone*) : My dear, you were perfectly right about the picture!

1ST WOMAN : But I couldn't have been. You said . . .

2ND WOMAN : Rubbish. Of course the picture represents Mary calling the cattle home, and always did!

1ST WOMAN : But you said it was a dimly sensed forest . . .

2ND WOMAN : That was only my nonsense, of course.

1ST WOMAN : But you said it was a symbolical exercise in abstract form . . .

2ND WOMAN : That was only my joke, of course. Can't you see I was pulling your leg?

1ST WOMAN : But you seemed so sincere and angry . . .

2ND WOMAN : Only my fun, I assure you. Of course, you must buy the picture for Christabel. Don't waste another moment. I didn't know anyone bought pictures in war-time!

1ST WOMAN : But neither Christabel nor I want an abstract French forest!

2ND WOMAN : Of course you don't. You want a charming representation of the delightful poem you used to recite—and I'm sure it can't have been so many years ago—well, you shall have it. I'll write " Mary Calls the Cattle Home " across the back. That will make it certain, won't it?

1ST WOMAN : But how dare you write across the back—oh, are all these pictures yours?

2ND WOMAN : Yes, but don't bother about that. Come to the desk at once!

4

1ST WOMAN : But I said the artist was an impossible woman !

2ND WOMAN : That was only your nonsense, of course. Can you still see the cows ?

1ST WOMAN : Yes, I can—but I said she dressed like a camouflaged aerodrome !

2ND WOMAN : That was only your joke, of course. Do the markings still look like water ?

1ST WOMAN : Yes, they do—but I said she smoked cigars and took drugs !

2ND WOMAN : I knew it was only your fun. Is the purple splotch still Mary ?

1ST WOMAN : It certainly is, but——

2ND WOMAN : That's all I want. Come to the desk *now* ! (*As she hurries the woman to the left*) You've no idea how wonderful it is to meet someone who *really* understands art. . . .

CHARLIE IS MY DARLING

On either side of the stage is a small table and on it a telephone. On either side of each table is a comfortable chair. If the room is small it does not matter if the tables are quite near each other, but the chairs should never be near each other ; they must always be right and left of each table.

[*The* 1ST WOMAN *enters from the right with a glass of water and a bottle of aspirins.*

1ST WOMAN : Now, shall I take an aspirin for my headache first, or ring up Mrs. Winterset ? (*Puts glass and bottle on table, sits down and contemplates telephone with some distaste.*) Better ring up first. If only they had not put us on the wretched dialling system ! I shall never understand it.

[*The* 2ND WOMAN *enters on the left with small dog under her arm.*

2ND WOMAN : At last some quietness. (*To dog*) Now, Charlie, darling, I want you to be very good and let mumsie get a nice little rest. (*Sits down with dog on her lap. Glances at the telephone.*) I hope to goodness no one calls me up for at least an hour. (*Looks at dog.*) The obedient lamb ! Asleep already. Mumsie will go to sleep too.

1ST WOMAN : Now, what's her number ! (*Takes small book out of her bag and consults it.*) Shanston three-five-eight. (*Puts book back in bag.*) Oh dear, I hope I shall get it with this new arrangement. Let me see if I can remember. (*Fingering dial*) Lift receiver. . . . (*Does so.*) . . . Yes, there is the low-pitched burr, burr . . . Insert finger . . . first letter . . . pull dial round and then let go. . . . I can't think why on earth one has to let go ; I should have thought it would spoil everything. . . . Shanston—that's just Sha, I suppose . . . S-H-A—now the number . . . Was it three-five-eight or five-three-eight ? Three-five-eight, five-three-eight, five-three-seven . . . Oh, dear ! Mustn't keep the thing waiting now it's purring . . . I'll risk five-three-eight. (*Dials.*)

2ND WOMAN (*opening her eyes as 'phone rings*) : I knew it ! Not a moment's peace all day long ! What a life ! (*To dog*) If only your poor mumsie weren't such an important person. (*Taking 'phone*) Yes, hullo, yes ?

1ST WOMAN : Is that you, dear ?

2ND WOMAN : Yes, I suppose it is. Who is it ?

1ST WOMAN : Hilda.

2ND WOMAN : Hilda. (*To dog*) I'm sure it's someone I'm supposed to know.

1ST WOMAN : What are you saying ?

2ND WOMAN : Nothing. Hilda, to be sure. I'm so glad you rang up. What a lovely day !

1ST WOMAN : I wanted to talk to you for a moment about the bazaar in the Church Hall.

2ND WOMAN : Is there a bazaar in the Church Hall ?

1ST WOMAN : Now, don't be funny, dear.

2ND WOMAN : Oh, was I being funny ?

1ST WOMAN : Well, I mean you're on the Committee, aren't you ?

2ND WOMAN : Oh, am I ? (*To dog*) Your mumsie's on so many committees she can't remember them all.

1ST WOMAN : And it's because you're on the Committee that I'm ringing up now.

2ND WOMAN : I'm sure it is. Please go on. If I can help in any way——

1ST WOMAN : Yes, you can, although it's something I shouldn't like to go any further. I mean, if the Vicar knew . . .

2ND WOMAN (*to dog*) : Poor mumsie's always getting confidences she doesn't want. (*To 'phone*) Please go on ; of course, the Vicar had better not know, whatever it is.

1ST WOMAN : He's such a dear, isn't he ? And at his age one mustn't worry him.

2ND WOMAN (*a little surprised*) : I don't call thirty-six old.

1ST WOMAN (*a little surprised*) : Why, he must be at least sixty ! However, don't let us waste time over the Vicar's age. I want to talk to you about Charlie.

2ND WOMAN (*again surprised*) : Charlie ? Do you really ? How curious ! (*To dog*) My pet, we're going to talk about *you* !

7

1st Woman : You see, Charlie's bound to be at the bazaar, isn't he?

2nd Woman : Well, if I go, he'll probably come also.

1st Woman : Then I see you've suffered as I have.

2nd Woman : Charlie has never caused me any suffering.

1st Woman : No, of course not. I beg your pardon, dear. You're above all that sort of thing.

2nd Woman : Above what sort of thing? Are you afraid of Charlie?

1st Woman : Yes, I am a little. I think quite a lot of us are.

2nd Woman : Well, I never knew that! Why?

1st Woman : Look at the reputation he's got.

2nd Woman : Reputation? Charlie? How on earth has Charlie got a reputation? What for?

1st Woman : I suppose you could call it audacity.

2nd Woman : I never thought Charlie was audacious. (*To dog*) What *have* you been hiding from mumsie, my precious?

1st Woman : But obviously he is. Just look at his face.

2nd Woman : His face? Wait a moment—— (*Examines dog's face*) Yes—I *think* I see what you mean.

1st Woman : But, naturally, it's not only his face. It's his most peculiar manner. Only the other night he became extremely—pestering—you know.

2nd Woman : Who should know if I don't?

1st Woman : Really? Then you'll be able to sympathise with me.

2nd Woman : Why should I sympathise? But I can't think where I was when he was pestering you.

1st Woman : Does that matter?

2nd Woman : Well, it wouldn't have happened had I been there.

1st Woman : Really!

8

2ND WOMAN : Of course. But it was only a sign of affection. You know how affectionate he is.

1ST WOMAN : I don't want that kind of affection.

2ND WOMAN : Don't you? I can't have enough of it.

1ST WOMAN : *Really?* Still, I believe everyone's talking about the way Charlie follows me about all over the place. Mother had to ask me if I knew.

2ND WOMAN : Rubbish! I shouldn't allow Charlie to follow you about all over the place.

1ST WOMAN : Wouldn't you? You do surprise me. How would you know, anyway?

2ND WOMAN : How could I help knowing? After all, Charlie belongs to me.

1ST WOMAN : *Belongs to you?*

2ND WOMAN : Well, if he doesn't, who does he belong to?

1ST WOMAN : Are you hinting at that girl—what was her name——?

2ND WOMAN : I'm not hinting at anyone. Why should I? I can't think how poor Charlie has upset you, but I'm sure it was only his play.

1ST WOMAN : Then he'd better play with someone else in the future.

2ND WOMAN : But the poor dear plays with everybody.

1ST WOMAN : You, included, apparently.

2ND WOMAN : Of course. We have the jolliest romps together.

1ST WOMAN : Good heavens! Well, I can't go on after that.

2ND WOMAN : But, of course, you must go on. What has all this to do with a bazaar?

1ST WOMAN : Well, you see, you're on the Committee, and so, of course, is Charlie.

2ND WOMAN (*laughing*) : Oh, that's rather sweet! Fancy Charlie on a Committee!

1ST WOMAN : I thought it funny, too, but, after what you've said, I scarcely imagined you would. But will you please use what I now see to be a remarkable influence, and stop Charlie from hanging round my stall and preventing me from getting on with my work and making people talk ?

2ND WOMAN : My dear girl, if I go to this bazaar and Charlie is with me, and I happen to be busy with something else, nothing will prevent Charlie from frisking and bounding all over the place. What if he does upset things ? You can't help loving him.

1ST WOMAN (*warmly*) : I can help it quite easily, and if he comes frisking and bounding in my direction, I shall call the Vicar. He is a most objectional creature and ought to have been expelled from the parish years ago !

2ND WOMAN : I don't in the least know what you're talking about ! Call the Vicar ? Expelled from the parish ? I don't know anything about this bazaar, although there are so many this summer that I've lost count. But I do know that Charlie is the dearest little rogue ever, completely harmless, anxious to love everyone, and my only joy and comfort. He must be bitterly hurt at hearing all this, the little poppet !

1ST WOMAN : The poppet ? The dearest little rogue ? Charlie ? Bitterly hurt at hearing—why, where *is* Charlie all this time ?

2ND WOMAN : Sitting on my lap, of course, looking up at me with the love-light in his eyes.

1ST WOMAN : OH ! You abandoned creature ! (*Slams down telephone, takes aspirin and drinks water hastily.*) Shocking !

2ND WOMAN (*sitting upright*) : Abandoned creature ? Disgraceful !

THE WOMEN (*together*) : Something must be done about this ! I will consult the Vicar without delay !

[*Both march out to battle.*

THE CURIO

SCENE.—*Ye Aunciente Crafte Shoppe.*

A counter at which sits the OWNER *of the shop : a dilapidated-looking female, wearing many beads and dressed in a kind of tea-gown which has obviously seen better days.*

[*Enter a* CUSTOMER, *fairly smartly dressed.*

OWNER (*rising*) : Oh, good morning, madam.

CUSTOMER : Good morning ; I thought I'd just pop in and have a look round.

OWNER : Of course, of course. Is there anything special you want ?

CUSTOMER : Well, not really—but anything interesting always attracts me.

OWNER : Naturally. Well, I have some very interesting things here to show you—and the best of it is they're all hand-made. That's so nice, isn't it ? What I mean is there's nothing mechanical about them. I always think mechanical things are so soul-destroying, don't you ?

CUSTOMER : Yes, I suppose I do. But these hand-made things are usually rather fragile—they break so easily, don't they ? I often think that one of the sure signs of a home-made thing is that it comes to pieces in your hand.

OWNER (*laughing uneasily*) : Oh, I'm sure that's just your fancy. Everything here is guaranteed to last for years if necessary. Now, take this delightful little velvet and taffeta pin-cushion, made in the shape of two doves of peace . . . charming, is it not, very ?

CUSTOMER : Well, yes, . . . but how puzzled they look, don't they ?

OWNER (*with brisk aplomb*) : Can you wonder at this moment, madam ? And here's another delicious little thing. A book-marker made of mackerel and shrimp skin ; so refreshingly nautical, is it not ? And should you want a rose-bowl or a butter-cooler, I have *innumerable*——

CUSTOMER : I don't think I want any of the everyday things

like rose-bowls, book-markers or pin-cushions. Have you got anything out of the ordinary? Anything really original?

OWNER : Why, yes, madam ; as it happens I have. (*Opening drawer in desk.*) Now here is something that I don't as a rule show to customers. In fact, it's not really for sale. I like to *cherish* it myself, you know. But, if I may say so, I can sense that you are a person of discrimination, and I'm sure you will love it at first sight. (*Holds up a tiny statue of Oriental aspect— see note at end of play.*) Isn't it enthralling? Doesn't it hold the gorgeous East in fee? You must admit it simply *reeks* of atmosphere !

CUSTOMER (*rather impressed*) : Well, it is a little strange, certainly. What exactly is it?

OWNER : It's the Palmanni God of good luck. The Palmannies are an almost extinct tribe, living, I believe, in the suburbs of Lassa, and their religion is entirely secret and most fascinating. There is probably not another little god like this in the whole of Europe. It belonged to my grandfather, who was a great traveller.

CUSTOMER : And has it brought you luck?

OWNER : Marvellously good luck—over and over again. That's why I haven't been able to bring myself to sell it up to now.

CUSTOMER : Yet you show it to me?

OWNER : Because, as I said, I realise you are the very person to appreciate its mystic qualities. And perhaps you are in need of a little good luck?

CUSTOMER : Oh, of course, I am. . . . Don't put it away. Let me look at it again. Yes ; I like its little face . . . distinctly.

OWNER : I knew you would. It has an expression which grows upon one, I assure you. (*Seems about to put it away again.*)

CUSTOMER : Yes, well, please don't put it away . . . I suppose . . . I suppose you have never really thought of parting with it?

OWNER : I have sometimes, because, of course, I try to be a business woman—but it doesn't suit me. I've not got the right temperament, as you see. And I always felt that one day someone would come who would be really worthy of this wonderful curio. However, perhaps . . . (*Opens drawer.*)

CUSTOMER : No, please let it stay out here. I am liking it more and more. . . . I suppose it would be very expensive . . . ? I really daren't splash money about nowadays . . . my husband would be furious . . . and yet, I've begun to feel I'd just love to have it.

OWNER : And, do you know, I'd love you to have it also, although, on the other hand, I shall hate parting with it. But I couldn't let it go at less than——

CUSTOMER : Go on—less than——!

OWNER : Less than a guinea.

CUSTOMER (*surprised*) : A guinea ? But how cheap—I mean ——

OWNER (*realising her mistake*) : Or two or three guineas, or five or even ten, of course, if not more !

CUSTOMER (*a trifle sharply*) : Come now, you said a guinea, I heard you. And that is certainly all I can afford—indeed, it is more than I ought to pay. I only came in for something quite simple.

OWNER : But think, madam, of the rarity of this object. The only one in Europe, I assure you.

CUSTOMER : Oh, quite, quite, but if you are going to suggest ten or more guineas, it is out of the question—and after all, I expect you'll be only too pleased to keep the curio yourself.

OWNER : Not at all, I've set my heart on you having it, madam.

CUSTOMER : But I can only pay your first price.

OWNER : Well, well, there are times when one must be generous. You shall have it for your guinea. (*Smiles winningly.*)

CUSTOMER : Well, it seems very good of you . . . and I'm sure I shall love it. I'll take it with me now.

OWNER : But of course ! I'll just fetch some wrappings. . . . (*Bustles out.*)

CUSTOMER (*taking up curio*) : A guinea—but even then, what will Herbert say ? It's rather sweet, and she says it's very rare. . . . I wonder what it's made of. . . . (*Is examining it closely when the head comes off.*) Oh, good heavens ! ! How awful ! What a calamity. And she said it brought good luck ! (*Jams head on again firmly.*) Stay on like that, for goodness' sake, and don't fall off until I've left. (*Pats her heart.*) What a terrible moment.

OWNER (*returning with papers, etc.*) : So sorry to have kept you waiting, but I wanted to find some really good paper for——

CUSTOMER : Oh, but I'm afraid that while you were away I thought things over, and have decided I really must not buy the curio after all.

OWNER : But how disappointing ! When I'd set my heart on you having it. How could you change your mind so quickly ? Why, it's turning your back on good luck !

CUSTOMER : It's no use. My husband would be furious at me spending so much money.

OWNER : Oh, I see. Well, can I meet you . . . instead of a guinea, say fifteen shillings ?

CUSTOMER : Oh, no, I couldn't possibly.

OWNER : Well, well,—ten and six ? I couldn't be more reasonable than that, could I ?

CUSTOMER : Indeed no, in fact, you surprise me. But I assure you I can't have it at all ; my husband wouldn't approve. I really have decided. I'll just take a look at those rose-bowls you mentioned. . . . (*Walks to back of stage apparently to inspect various objects.*)

OWNER (*looking after her and frowning*) : Awkward fool ! (*Takes up curio and gives it a little shake.*) Just as I was hoping to get you off to-day . . . (*At which point the head comes off.*) Good gracious! What on earth made it do that ? (*Jamming the head on again.*) Stay there, for heaven's sake. She must have you now. (*To* CUSTOMER) Ahem . . . ! I really can't see you leave the shop with so ordinary a thing as a rose-bowl. You shall have this priceless mascot for eight and six.

CUSTOMER : No, no, I assure you . . .

OWNER : Well, really—seven and six—five shillings, there !

CUSTOMER (*astounded*) : Five shillings ? But surely it cannot be as valuable as you say if you are willing to let it go at that ?

OWNER : I assure you, madam, it is one of the most valuable objects in my shop. It is only because I feel an innate sympathy——

CUSTOMER : Innate sympathy ? Rubbish ! I believe you'd let it go for half a crown if I stopped long enough.

OWNER : Indeed, madam, you offend me. The mascot is not only valuable but full of exquisite workmanship. (*With sinister intention*) If you doubt me, take it in your hands and examine it yourself.

CUSTOMER (*hastily*) : Oh, no, I'd rather not do that !

OWNER : But why not ? Seeing is believing, madam. Hold it up and have a good look at it.

CUSTOMER : Hold it up yourself.

OWNER : No, if you don't mind, I'd rather not.

CUSTOMER : But why not ?

OWNER : It—it might not be lucky. It's a strange object, and . . .

CUSTOMER : Well, I certainly will not touch it, and you seem afraid to—I expect, like all hand-made things, it's not safe to touch.

OWNER : I think you are becoming most unfair. What do you think would happen if I touched it ?

CUSTOMER (*taking a risk*) : Probably its head would come off.

OWNER (*confused*) : Its head . . . madam ? Come off . . . its head ?

CUSTOMER (*enjoying this*) : Yes, that's it. I've guessed rightly. If you touch it, its head will come off.

OWNER (*with sudden intuition*) : And may I ask, madam, *why* you are so certain of that ?

CUSTOMER (*her turn to be confused*) : Well . . . what I mean is, it looks as if its head might come off—doesn't it ?

OWNER : That was not my impression when I first took it out of this drawer . . . but now (*examining the figure*) . . . yes, madam, it would be interesting to know why you are so certain its head will come off.

CUSTOMER : If it comes to that, it would be interesting to know why *you* were so confused when I first suggested that its head might come off.

OWNER : You knew it would.

CUSTOMER : And you knew that I knew that you knew——

OWNER : I knew that I knew that I knew you knew that I knew that I knew that you knew——

BOTH (*violently*) : In any case, you knew ! !

CUSTOMER (*walking to the door*) : This is ridiculous ! Good morning.

OWNER (*quickly hiding the statue and taking from the drawer another little figure precisely similar*) : One moment, madam. (*The* CUSTOMER *turns.*) I should like to prove to you that you are mistaken. You will note that I can turn this little god up and down, hold it in any direction, play with it as much as I like, and the head does NOT come off !

CUSTOMER (*not to be caught*) : Didn't I hear you take something out of the drawer when my back was turned ?

OWNER : Really, madam, if I may say so, you have one of the most suspicious natures I have ever met. I only wish to demonstrate to you that this little statue——

CUSTOMER : Let me see. (*Takes hold of curio and examines it.*) It certainly seems all right now. (*In twisting it about she suddenly drops it.*) Oh, oh, now it's gone altogether !

OWNER (*rising in assumed wrath*) : Really, madam, this is too much. First you offer to buy this valuable curio, then you refuse to buy it and hint that it is broken, and then, when I prove to you that this is not so, you snatch it from me and actually break it ! (*Going round to pick up the fragments.*) Let me inform you that this is really serious. A most valuable object, the only one of its kind in Europe. . . .

CUSTOMER (*running to desk and opening drawer*) : The only one of its kind ? (*Looks in drawer*) Ah, I thought so ! (*Takes out five other little statues, each one a replica of the first.*) Here's a perfect nest of them ! Very rare ? A guinea ? No wonder you brought down the price. (*Quickly arranges them in a row on the*

16

desk.) If I were you I should put them in the window, labelled twopence. There'd be a profit even then. Good morning !

[*She sweeps out of the shop, leaving the* OWNER *speechless.*

Curtain.

NOTE.—There is no need for the little gods used in this play to be elaborate, difficult properties. The simplest shapes in clay, papier-maché, plasticine, or even cloth will suffice ; if possible they should be brightly coloured. The one which is smashed can be dropped behind the desk and the noise of breaking simulated.

IN CONFIDENCE

CHARACTERS

THE YOUNG GIRL.
THE GOOD LADY.

SCENE.—*The lounge of an hotel.*

The YOUNG GIRL *is fairly pretty, rather pert—and becomingly dressed. The* GOOD LADY *is a mass of sentiment and oppressive wisdom. She sits in the centre, sewing some impossible garment ; there is a somewhat smaller and lower chair on her right. The* YOUNG GIRL *has evidently just entered.*

LADY (*looking up*) : Ah, my dear Christobel, I am so very glad to see you. Now, do come and rest a little—all this walking about must be so bad for you.

CHRISTOBEL : I assure you, my dear Mrs. Scantlebury, I'm not in the least tired. With this air, I could walk all day and not feel done up.

LADY (*smiling benignly*) : Ah, you young people always talk like that. But there *is* such a thing as tiredness, even at your age. Now, do rest, dear ; come, sit on that chair beside me. I've been wanting to have a talk with you so much !

CHRISTOBEL (*a little surprised*) : With me ? What on earth for ? (*Sitting down.*) I mean, my life's not particularly interesting, you know.

LADY (*seriously*) : My dear, the life of any young, growing thing is interesting. I find the lives of all the young things around me enthralling. I watch them all day long, and you cannot realise how I *yearn* to help and comfort them ! There is nothing I cannot understand ; their worries and difficulties are never hidden from me. Besides, your dear mother asked me to keep an eye on you while you were here, so, naturally, I take the keenest interest in you.

CHRISTOBEL : Well, that's very good of you, I'm sure. But I'm afraid there is nothing extraordinary about my life. I'm a perfectly ordinary girl.

LADY (*laying down her sewing and clasping her hands over her knees*) : I often think that no one is perfectly ordinary. Every-

18

one has a story, you know, if one can only find it out. And how much everyone needs comfort ! I should like to devote my whole life to helping young friends.

CHRISTOBEL : Well, I'm sure that's quite sweet of you. But suppose they haven't any troubles and don't need helping ?

LADY : My dear, we all have troubles ; we all need help. The young, especially. Now, you, with that pretty face of yours . . .

CHRISTOBEL (*not displeased*) : Well . . . yes . . . go on.

LADY : That winning manner . . . your dear father also has winning manners ; you must have inherited them.

CHRISTOBEL : I wish everyone thought so pleasantly about me. Please go on.

LADY : Ah, my dear, but these gifts have to be paid for. The gods exact a price for their favours, you know.

CHRISTOBEL : Do they ? How uncomfortable of them. But they haven't inflicted many worries on me, yet.

LADY : Now, you know, I wonder about that. I so often watch people's faces ; I've been told I've a special flair for psychology, and I think it must be true. And as I watched your face at dinner last night, it seemed to me that there were some lines of anxiety that had no right to be there. And I felt—oh, could I but help a little !

CHRISTOBEL : At dinner last night ? Oh, yes, I know what I was thinking about. But how clever of you to notice it.

LADY : My dear, I have made it my life's work to notice things. And, you see, I was right. You were anxious, worried . . . now, confess you were.

CHRISTOBEL : Well, yes, I was—but I am certain it will all come right.

LADY : Ah, yes, we always hope things will come all right, but how much do we do to *make* them come right ? That's where the advice of an older friend is so invaluable. To be able to go to someone, older and wiser, and *in confidence* to pour out the sorrows of the heart—what a truly beautiful thing !

CHRISTOBEL (*a little restive*) : But I wouldn't call this a sorrow of the heart.

19

LADY (*gently*) : We will call it whatever you like, dear, but, in any case, you need tell me, oh, so little about it. I can guess.

CHRISTOBEL (*surprised*) : Can you really ? And what do you guess ?

LADY : Well, to begin with, it concerns a friend—a *man* friend, does it not ?

CHRISTOBEL (*smiling*) : Well, yes, that is true enough ; it does.

LADY : But, of course ! At your age it could be nothing else. But I don't think you should smile like that. You mustn't be heartless. Oh, the lives I've known broken up by heartlessness.

CHRISTOBEL : But it's something he'll easily get over.

LADY : Oh, my dear, don't say that ! Don't ever say that ! I know men ; I know how deeply disappointment can burn and fester. Say what you like, men are super-sensitive creatures. I know how badly they can take the loss of that they have cherished.

CHRISTOBEL : Yes, but it's so silly of him to go about cherishing things.

LADY : My dear, it's not for you to say that, is it ? Come, come, you must try to understand. After all, the whole affair was a compliment, wasn't it ?

CHRISTOBEL : Well, in a way—I say, how much do you really know about it all ?

LADY : Everything, my dear, *everything*. I have often been told I am rather clairvoyant, and there is a great deal in it. I'm probably clairvoyant now ; in fact, I'm sure I am. And remember, my confidence is sacred ! You cannot surprise or shock me, and there is *nothing* I do not understand. Alas, your story is not a new story my dear . . . young girls are careless . . .

CHRISTOBEL : That's just it, I have been careless.

LADY (*patting her arm*) : I know, I know. And it is much that you admit it. Ah me ! I was the same at your age. Such a careless, feckless, feather-headed little darling !—And he, of course, was hurt ?

CHRISTOBEL : Not yet, but he will be. Of course, the thing to do is to get another.

LADY : *Another ?* Oh, my dear, " another " as you call it, usually complicates things dreadfully !

CHRISTOBEL : The question is, would he ever find out ?

LADY : Find out ? But, of course he will. The change——

CHRISTOBEL : But I'm hoping he wouldn't notice any change.

LADY : Sweet child, how innocent you are ! Oh, I'm glad I spoke in time. Believe me, men are terribly quick to notice things . . . in fact, it's perfectly amazing what they *do* notice once their interest is roused. I *know* !

CHRISTOBEL : Well, if that is so, it's a shocking nuisance.

LADY : My dear, you must not be so flippant over sacred matters.

CHRISTOBEL : Sacred ?

LADY : It's sacred to him, isn't it ?

CHRISTOBEL : Well, I'm so afraid it may be.

LADY : Ah, now we're getting nearer to the heart of the matter ! My poor child, you're afraid. . . .

CHRISTOBEL : Yes, I am. You see, I particularly don't want to go to him and tell him about it.

LADY : I know, I know. (*Wipes away a tear.*) Oh, these cruel complications ! It is all inexpressibly sad, but it must be faced. You must summon up all your courage, and mind you when I say all, I mean *all*, and confess the truth.

CHRISTOBEL : And then he heaves something at me.

LADY (*startled*) : He would never be such a brute ?

CHRISTOBEL : You don't know my cousin Geoffrey.

LADY : Your cousin ? Oh dear, that makes it all the more necessary you should clear the matter up without delay. I know I'm old-fashioned, but marriage between——

CHRISTOBEL : But there is no question of marriage.

LADY : None !

CHRISTOBEL : None whatever. That is the last thing we should think of.

21

LADY (*enjoying herself*) : Dear me, tut, tut ! This is even worse than I supposed ! Then perhaps, after all, it may be wise if you lose no time in getting what you call " another."

CHRISTOBEL : Yes, but it will be much brighter and glossier and look so awfully new. . . . that's what worries me.

LADY : Glossy ? New ? What do you mean ?

CHRISTOBEL : Well, penguins do when they're fresh, don't they ?

LADY : Penguins ? Is that a slang term for a new friend ? Still, there is no doubt that you must have the courage to go to this cousin of yours—whom I'm afraid is no gentleman——

CHRISTOBEL : That's what I tell him. And what do I say ?

LADY : You say to him, " Geoffrey, romance has come, romance has gone. I have another——"

CHRISTOBEL : Penguin.

LADY : My dear, this flippancy will ruin your life. Geoffrey will never understand that.

CHRISTOBEL : Oh, won't he just.

LADY : Why, do you call him a penguin too ?

CHRISTOBEL : Of course not, the silly josser.

LADY : My dear, you must remember that Geoffrey loves you.

CHRISTOBEL : I'd give him a good clout if I thought he did !

LADY : But everything points to——

CHRISTOBEL : Just because he lent me a silly book that he said had valuable associations——

LADY : A book——?

CHRISTOBEL : A sixpenny penguin " History of the World " he'd bought last year, and lent me as a favour—and now I've gone and lost it—oh, but what have you been thinking ?

LADY : Thinking ? I've been doing my best to help you.

CHRISTOBEL : To help me ? You seem to imagine I'm in the middle of some mysterious love affair with my idiotic cousin !

What a mind you must have ! If this is clairvoyance, please do not become clairvoyant again. Love, marriage, " have the courage to tell him ! " My dear Mrs. Scantlebury, I have the courage to tell you you're a sentimental busybody ! Good morning. (*Marches out.*)

LADY (*astounded*) : Oh, how shocking . . . ! ! (*Recovering a little*) But perhaps she did not tell me the truth. . . . In fact, I'm sure she did not. I always know *everything* !

[*Much comforted, she nods and smiles to herself as the* CURTAIN *falls.*

BELINDA AND THE GOOD FAIRY

CHARACTERS

THE FAIRY MELLILUNE.
BELINDA.

BELINDA *enters on the right, immersed in a solemn-looking book. She crosses the stage slowly, pausing twice to consult notes at the end of the book. As she nears an old tree-stump which is placed on the left of the stage, she looks at it and decides to sit down. Just as she is about to sit she notices something on the trunk.*

BELINDA (*examining trunk*) : A lady-bird—I should say, a coleopterous insect. I will not sit on it. (*Takes envelope she has been using for a book-marker out of the book, and scooping up the insect, places it at the back of the stump. As soon as she has done this, the* GOOD FAIRY *rises quickly from behind the tree-trunk and beams at her.*)

FAIRY : Oh, thank you, thank you, a thousand times thank you !

BELINDA : Well, really ! May I ask who you are ?

FAIRY : Can't you guess ?

BELINDA : Indeed, no. I presume you are on your way to some pageant, or, possibly, an open-air performance of " The Dream."

FAIRY : Of course not, my dear. Surely it is obvious I'm one of the good fairies.

BELINDA : Nonsense.

FAIRY : Oh, but I am. I'm the good fairy Mellilune, and I am full of gratitude to you.

BELINDA : I fail to follow you, especially when you speak of gratitude. What have I done ?

FAIRY : A kind action, that is all. Just a kind action, but it rescued me from a horrible enchantment.

BELINDA : All this is rather singular. What enchantment ?

FAIRY : Don't you realise I was the lady-bird you so tenderly scooped up and placed on the ground ?

BELINDA : How absurd you are ! How could you possibly have been a tiny insect ?

FAIRY : My dear, I was taking a little stroll when I most unfortunately met my greatest enemy, the witch Horribrand. We had not seen each other for years, but no sooner had she set eyes on me than she shrieked a nasty spell at me, and I was so confused that I couldn't remember the counterspell. So, in the twinkling of an eye, I found myself transformed into a lady-bird, while the hag, with horrible chuckles, told me I should remain in that predicament until someone passed who did me an act of kindness. Wasn't it awful ! Fortunately, Horribrand had hardly vanished before you appeared, and by your thoughtfulness rescued me at once. And how grateful I am ! You shall be rewarded speedily, I assure you.

BELINDA : Look here, as far as I'm concerned, you're talking absolute nonsense. All this chatter about metamorphosis and witches—there are no witches nowadays—and such things don't happen. You—well, to use a common and rather distressing idiom, you're pulling my leg.

FAIRY : Indeed, I'm not. Dear little girl——

BELINDA : I beg your pardon ?

FAIRY : Dear little girl—you are a dear little girl, you know.

BELINDA : Oh, am I ? It's a long time since anyone presumed to call me that.

FAIRY : But you must be a dear little girl or you wouldn't have behaved as you did. And now you shall learn that acts of kindness *never* go unrewarded, especially if done to a fairy. Listen ; as a reward I will give you a wish.

BELINDA : A wish ? Now, what do you mean ?

FAIRY : One big, beautiful wish. You shall ask for whatever you like, and whatever it is you shall have it—or it will happen —it depends on the nature of the wish, of course. Now, isn't that a marvellous reward for being a good little girl ?

BELINDA : I'm sorry, but I cannot follow any of this. I am completely unconscious of having done anything particularly meritorious ; I am considerably perplexed by your appearance, to say nothing of your curiously familiar manner, and when you offer me the instant fulfilment of some wish—I believe I am right in supposing that is what you do offer? (FAIRY *nods*)—well, I'm sorry to be rude, but you're taxing my credulity too far.

FAIRY : Now, now, it doesn't become a little girl to be so sceptical and suspicious. Haven't you a saying—" You never know your luck " ?

BELINDA : I believe in flippant conversation such things are sometimes said.

FAIRY : And sometimes it's true. Just now, for instance. You do not know your luck.

BELINDA : I'm afraid you're talking wildly. Jokes are jokes, of course, although, personally, I do not care for them, but do consider what you're saying. It's all so preposterous.

FAIRY : But you must have heard of this kind of thing occurring to good little girls before ?

BELINDA : My dear woman, I left off reading the deleterious fables in which such things are spoken of at the age of six. I found it better for my mental balance.

FAIRY : But aren't you rejoiced to discover that they were true after all ? That you are now one of those good little girls who have had this tremendous event happen to them ?

BELINDA : Even supposing, theoretically, that what you say is true—which I do not for a moment admit—would it be such a tremendous event ?

FAIRY : But, of course, it would be. Think of what it means. You can have just what you want. Isn't that a wonderful thought ?

BELINDA : I cannot say it is. To have just what they want has never been good for anyone. Think of Nero, think of Napoleon, think of the *Czars*—— !

FAIRY : Why waste time thinking of disagreeable people ? Concentrate on your own happiness. Now, what is the wish to be ? I am quite ready ! (*Strikes attitude and beams on her again.*)

BELINDA : You must be well aware that if I really gave my attention to the subject, it would land you in the most impossible situation.

FAIRY (*still beaming*) : Try me and see.

BELINDA : You wouldn't smile like that if I took you at your word.

FAIRY : But of course I should, dear.

BELINDA : Even if I asked for the nationalisation of banks, transport and agriculture ?

FAIRY (*surprised*) : You surely wouldn't require anything so —peculiar ?

BELINDA : Could you do it if I asked you ?

FAIRY : Well—it would be——

BELINDA : Don't hedge. Could you do it ?

FAIRY (*trying to smile*) : Well, it seems—a little unusual, doesn't it ?

BELINDA : That means you couldn't do it. I thought so Suppose I demanded the liquidation of the bourgeoisie and the dictatorship of the proletariat ?

FAIRY : But—my dear—consider——

BELINDA : Could you do it ?

FAIRY : Well—it might be a little—difficult.

BELINDA : Can you eradicate the financial oligarchy, abolish private property, and put an end to the deviations of the falsely so-called intelligentsia ?

FAIRY : There you go again—darling—no one ever heard——

BELINDA : *Can you do it ?*

FAIRY : I might have a *try*, of course, but——

BELINDA : You see, your foolish promises fall to pieces the moment they are tested.

FAIRY : Not at all. Had you asked for a lot of money, or a huge box of sweets, or some pretty dresses, or a handsome Prince——

BELINDA : That will do. Your ideas are becoming *risqué* and subversive.

FAIRY (*shocked*) : How can you say so ?

27

BELINDA : But I do say so. My father earns an honest living ; I gave up sweets years ago ; my dresses are sufficient for my means ; and I need hardly say a handsome Prince would be ideologically repulsive to me. Your rewards are sordid, vulgar, and completely bourgeois ; and when I ask you to do something really *big*, you fail, miserably.

FAIRY : I'm not sure I should fail exactly, but there might be —complications.

BELINDA : So I imagine. Well, I don't believe in you and have not believed in you from the first. You're nothing but an old impostor who has had the impudence to try and hoodwink me with mediaeval bunkum.

FAIRY (*enraged*) : You really are a dreadful little girl ! If this is the modern child, the world is lost. You ought to have a mind as innocent as a daisy-chain, and ask for pretty, charming things, but instead—why, I expect even the book you're reading is not what any nice little girl should read. (*Takes book and reads title*) " Karl Marx "—goodness knows who he is, but I know how to deal with him. (*Is about to throw the book away.*)

BELINDA (*snatching it from her*) : You rude, silly old woman ! You ought to know we have progressed far beyond all this rubbish nowadays. Interrupting my morning studies with such tosh ! Fairy, are you ? Lady-bird, were you ? Insects are far more use in the modern world than fairies. I wish you *were* a lady-bird !

[*With a shriek, the* FAIRY *vanishes behind the trunk. For a moment* BELINDA *is startled. Then she recovers herself.*

Well, that's got rid of her. (*Peering into the wings*) She must have run away amazingly rapidly. I can't see her. Now for a good read ! (*Is about to sit on the trunk when she is surprised by what she sees on it.*) Good gracious ! Another lady-bird . . . ! or . . . surely not ? ? ? (*Is about to scoop up the insect with the envelope when she stops.*) No . . . better not be rash ! (*Contemplates the trunk for a moment.*) No, I don't believe it ! I can't believe it ! (*Opens book resolutely.*) Karl Marx is the only cure for this sort of thing ! (*Marches off, diligently reading the book.*)

SAFE AREA

CHARACTERS

1ST VISITOR.
2ND VISITOR.
THE TRIPPER.

The SCENE *is a shelter at a seaside resort. While it will be an advantage if the shelter is to some extent suggested, this is not necessary. All that is necessary is a long and high seat, closed in at each end, with, in the centre, a partition high enough to conceal the occupants on either side from each other.*

When the CURTAIN *rises this seat is empty, but immediately afterwards a* TRIPPER *enters (evidently of the cheaper sort), up for the day. She is wearing a remarkable hat and costume, and carries a dilapidated handbag. She sits down on the right-hand side of the partition, and surveys the view with satisfaction. At which moment two fashionably dressed* VISITORS *saunter in on the left.*

1ST VISITOR (*as they enter*) : As I was saying, dear Lady Harriet had, of course, an answer ready. In that beautiful, clear voice of hers—oh, here's a seat. Don't you think a little rest is indicated ?

2ND VISITOR : Indeed, I do. Dear Doctor Bartram always says I must rest as much as possible.

1ST VISITOR : Bartram ? (*As they sit down on the left*) Any relation to old Sir Hugh Bartram of Dopplefield ?

2ND VISITOR : I've really no idea, but, of course, as he is a most distinguished man he may be. " Dear Mrs. Bingham-Longton," he said on parting, " rest is what you need. Rest and nourishment. Eat little but often." So I always carry a few diminutive sandwiches with me, and a thermos full of coffee (*displaying a very decorative basket which appears to be bursting with food*), and when I feel tired I sit down and have a tiny, tiny repast. I do hope you'll join me.

1ST VISITOR : Too kind of you.

2ND VISITOR : Not at all. It's so delightful to meet someone of one's own—well, *type*, when away.

29

1st Visitor : Indeed yes. I must say I expected to meet more decent people in such a safe area. Why, if we hadn't had the sense to speak to each other at breakfast, I do believe there would have been no one fit to talk to the whole day long ! Shall we rest here until the town clock strikes eleven and then have that little repast you so kindly offered ?

2nd Visitor : That will be delightful; especially as it must be nearly eleven now. Meanwhile, do go on with your anecdote about Lady Harriet. I am *so* interested.

1st Visitor : Well, Lady Harriet, who is just a *wee* bit unconventional at times, rose, and in a loud, clear voice——

[*The* Tripper, *now thoroughly at home with her surroundings, puts her feet up on the seat, preparatory to having a doze.*

2nd Visitor : Did you hear a strange noise ?

1st Visitor : Yes, but it's sure to be nothing at all alarming here.

2nd Visitor : And isn't that a blessing ! Such a safe area ! No disturbances whatever, I am told.

1st Visitor : I suppose that's why the terms at the hotel are so terribly high.

2nd Visitor : We mustn't complain. It's worth it. Think of the days and days of perfect peace and quietness . . .

1st Visitor : Long, long talks . . .

2nd Visitor (*looking at basket*) : Constant nourishment . . .

1st Visitor (*feeling more and more comfortable*) : Indeed, yes. We can forget the war . . .

2nd Visitor : I suppose we ought not to do that *entirely*, ought we ?

1st Visitor : Oh, no, of course not—but still, in a safe area . . .

2nd Visitor : That's what I keep saying to myself. Safe area —safe area——

[*The* Tripper *shifts her feet about.*
Now, what was that ?

1ST VISITOR : Merely the incoming tide. Let us return to Lady Harriet. As I was saying, in a loud, clear voice she——

[*The* TRIPPER *snores loudly.*

2ND VISITOR : Listen ! I am sure that is something surging through the air !

1ST VISITOR : More probably the wind. I remember one night at old Lady Shoreham's delightful place in Surrey, the wind was so tremendous that she——

[TRIPPER, *feeling uncomfortable, sits up, takes the handbag and gives it a shake.*

2ND VISITOR : I'm certain that was an explosion right out at sea !

1ST VISITOR : Well, provided it was far enough out, it doesn't concern us, does it ? As I say, thank heaven for the navy.

2ND VISITOR : I do so admire your coolness. Please go on about Lady Harriet.

[TRIPPER, *meanwhile, puts the handbag under her head and tries to sleep again.*

1ST VISITOR : Well, as I was saying, she was not the one to stand any nonsense—the Deverals never have stood any non-sense, you know——

2ND VISITOR : No, indeed ; of course not !

1ST VISITOR : So, in a loud, clear voice she——

[TRIPPER, *who has taken the handbag from under her head, now sees that the clasp is broken. She gives a whistle of dismay.*

2ND VISITOR (*clutching* 1ST VISITOR) : Listen !

1ST VISITOR (*a little disturbed*) : I certainly don't understand that.

2ND VISITOR : I do. It was a whistling bomb somewhere, I'm certain.

1ST VISITOR : But there was no bang.

2ND VISITOR : Probably delayed action.

1ST VISITOR (*aggrieved*) : But this is a safe area—all the adver-tisements said so !

2ND VISITOR : Well, I don't like it at all.

1ST VISITOR (*rousing herself*) : Still, it's our duty to carry on as usual.

2ND VISITOR : But not while *they* carry on as usual, surely ?

1ST VISITOR (*rallying her*) : My dear, we must try to cultivate courage. How well I remember dear old General Higson saying to me, " Lucy, my sweetest "—he'd known me from childhood—" Lucy, my——"

[*The* TRIPPER *shakes out the contents of her handbag—which can be as extraordinary as the producer or the kind of audience permits—and examines them intently. A piece of old newspaper in which some of them have been wrapped falls to the front.*

2ND VISITOR : Look, look !

1ST VISITOR (*gazing up into the sky*) : Where ? I can't see anything. Not even a sea-gull.

2ND VISITOR : Not in the sky. Look on the ground. They've been dropping leaflets.

1ST VISITOR : Good gracious ! I believe they have.

2ND VISITOR : I'm sure we ought to pick it up at once. It may be *most* important !

1ST VISITOR : Leave everything to me. I'll get it.

[*Very gingerly, with frequent looks towards the sky, she advances towards the paper. Then with her sunshade she tries to hook the paper towards her. Her preoccupation with this task will prevent her seeing the* TRIPPER *even if the paper has not fallen far enough in front.*

2ND VISITOR (*clapping her hands as* 1ST VISITOR *manages at last to hook the paper*) : How brave you are ! I should have been frightened to touch it.

1ST VISITOR : Ah, but you see we're all in the front line now. (*Inspecting paper*) I'd better read it to you. (*Takes out of her bag an impressive pair of horn-rimmed glasses, puts them on and reads*) " Have you that middle-aged feeling ? Is your tongue slightly furred ? Do you suffer from a sense of fullness ? No, nothing serious. Try Milko-Bilko." (*They look at each other.*) Extraordinary !

2ND VISITOR : It's only their devilish cleverness. You may be sure there's a hidden meaning behind it. It ought to be taken to the police at once.

1ST VISITOR (*regretfully*) : But we were getting so comfortable. Besides, there's our elevenses. (*Glances fondly at the basket ; then, firmly, puts the paper and the glasses in her bag.*) We'll have some food first, dear. It will strengthen us for dealing with the police. As I was saying. Lady Harriet in a loud, clear voice——

[*The* TRIPPER *tries to mend the clasp of the handbag by hitting it rapidly with her hand.*

2ND VISITOR (*clutching* 1ST VISITOR) : Distant gunfire !

1ST VISITOR (*half rising*) : I believe you may be right !

2ND VISITOR (*completely upset*) : We ought not to stop here, right on the front ! Most exposed ! Fancy all this in a safe area. It just shows what we're coming to !

1ST VISITOR (*shaken, but endeavouring to remain cool and collected*) : My dear, we must really stay put. Obviously that gunfire is far away, and as I said, it doesn't matter much what happens provided it happens in the distance. Come, come, as I was telling you, Lady Harriet took one step forward, and in a loud, clear voice——

[*The* TRIPPER, *in an attempt to mend the clasp, puts the bag on the ground and jumps on it.*

2ND VISITOR (*springing up with the other* VISITOR) : A bomb ! A bomb ! And quite near !

1ST VISITOR : Yes, indeed, we must fly at once !

[*They hurry towards the left.*

[*The* TRIPPER *jumps once more on the handbag.*

2ND VISITOR (*as they run*) : Oh ! ! ! And to think they called this a safe area !

[*They disappear as fast as their dignity allows them. The basket of food is left.*

TRIPPER (*surveying the handbag and noting with satisfaction that her efforts have actually mended the clasp*) : Well, that's that. (*Comes to the front ; sees the basket.*) O-o-o ! And just when I was ready for lunch ! It's almost too good to be true !

[*She seizes the basket, and with that in one hand and the bag in the other, walks out quickly, in triumph, on the right.*

[*A clock strikes eleven as the* CURTAIN *falls.*

THE HOSPICE

A small shelter is seen crowded with women wearing raincoats and carrying umbrellas. They are led by two rather austere ladies, Miss Sarah Timson *and* Miss Gladys Simpson. *All are gazing anxiously out of the shelter, and a general atmosphere of dampness prevails.*

Miss Timson : Well, despite the weather we've managed to reach the top !

Miss Simpson : And it wasn't such a climb after all, Sarah.

Miss Timson : Don't be silly, Gladys, of course it was. I declare I'm quite tired out, and so (*turning to the* Women) I'm sure are you all. Aren't you ?

Several Women : Yes, miss ; it was proper tiring, it was.

A Woman : You get more tired when it rains, I allus think.

Miss Timson : Yes, I'm sure there's a good deal in that, Mrs. Martin—and it really is a pity that we have encountered such bad weather on our outing.

A Woman : But doesn't it allus rain on an outing ?

Miss Timson (*rallying her*) : Now, Mrs. Bracegirdle, I can't allow that. You really are exaggerating.

A Woman : Nay, she's not. As soon as an outing starts, it rains. That's the rule. Why, I've never missed bringing my umbrella and my mac on an outing yet, and allus been glad of 'em.

Women : Ay, and allus will be !

Miss Timson : Come, come, this will never do ! Naughty pessimism ! It's enough to make it rain all the harder.

Miss Simpson : Still, there's something in what they say, Sarah. Remember last year when we went to Phantom Abbey?

Women : Ay, that was a proper soak, that was !

Miss Timson : I'm amazed at you all. Especially you, Gladys, encouraging such depression. What if it has rained ? Haven't we always been equal to the occasion ? Look at to-day.

35

Undaunted, we took the train, undaunted we strode steadily forward, until we reached our goal—the famous Hospice.

A WOMAN : What is a hospice, Miss ?

MISS TIMSON : Well, it was originally built by the dear old monks as a place of refuge for——

A WOMAN : I don't hold with monks at all.

A WOMAN : Evangelical I've always been, and evangelical I intend to remain.

MISS TIMSON : But all this was ages and ages ago.

A WOMAN (*firmly*) : That makes no difference to me, Miss.

MISS TIMSON : Well, anyway, the little building we're in now was put up only a few years ago as a place for rest and refreshment——

[*The* WOMEN *cheer up considerably.*

A WOMAN : Refreshment'll just suit us, Miss.

A WOMAN : I could do with a nice cup o' tea.

WOMEN : Ay, and so could we all !

A WOMAN : But I don't see no refreshment rooms.

MISS TIMSON : Of course not. I meant refreshment of the soul.

WOMEN (*depressed*) : Oh, did yer. . . .

A WOMAN : But supposing there *had* bin a tea-room. . . .

A WOMAN (*whispering*) : Or a pub . . .

WOMEN : Ay ! *Supposing !*

MISS TIMSON : Now, we must not think of such places. I'm astonished at you ! We must be patient. Organization is all important, even on an outing. That means we must follow our programme exactly. Tea is at the end of the excursion when we get back to the town in an hour's time.

MISS SIMPSON : I'm sure it didn't take us an hour to get here, Sarah.

MISS TIMSON : My dear Gladys, it must have done.

A WOMAN : Seemed more like two hours with feet like I've got.

A Woman : And now we've got here we can't see nothing.

Miss Timson : Well, I admit the mist is a pity, but in these mountainous districts it is so often like this. But, of course, when it does clear it will be *marvellous* ! And there's certainly a faint wind stirring, so that's hopeful.

Miss Simpson : Probably blowing up for worse weather.

Women : Ay, that'll be it, Miss !

Miss Timson : Now, now, I implore you to cast away all this gloom. Gladys, you really ought to try and be a better example to the others. We've much to enjoy, even at this moment. For instance, did you ever breathe better or more invigorating air ? Let us all take deep breaths of it. Now, follow me. When I say *Ah*, expel all the air from your lungs. Come along, it's so good for you. Now ; one—two—three—*Ah ! !*

[*The result of this is an explosion of coughing and choking among the* Women.

A Woman : This'll fair do for me, Miss.

A Woman (*a miracle of health*) : You don't realise how dangerous these breathing games can be to us delicate ones, Miss.

A Woman : Any case, it makes me drier than ever.

Women : Ay, it does us, too.

A Woman : Didn't someone say at the station that we passed the " Traveller's Rest Tea-rooms " on the way up ?

Several Women (*eagerly*) : Ay, stationmaster said so when Miss asked him the way.

Miss Timson : Now, it's quite useless thinking of tea-rooms and " Traveller's Rests " up here. We're miles away from such places ; far, far from the madding crowd, like somebody or other on a peak in Darien. Before us is a most wonderful view ; all around us are huge, glorious mountains . . .

A Woman : What's the good of views and mountains if we can't see 'em ?

A Woman : Who wants to see 'em, anyway ? What we want's a bit of comfort.

A Woman : Can't think why an outing's allus in the country.

A Woman : Nor I. Country's bad enough, even when it doesn't rain.

A Woman (*explaining to the others*) : You see, there's nothing *homely* about the country. In town you can get a cup o' tea when you're parched, but the country's nothing but fields and fields and trees and trees, and when there's a mountain planked in the middle of 'em it's worse than ever.

A Woman : Nasty, frowning things, mountains.

Miss Timson : You really *must* try to enjoy yourselves. The country's truly wonderful. I'm sure that deep down in your hearts you all feel that.

A Woman : Deep down in my heart I want a cup o' tea.

Women : Ay, that's what we want !

Miss Timson : I wish you'd understand that's quite impossible until we get away from here. And you really should try and appreciate the beauties of the country more. What is it Wordsworth says ?—" I wandered, lonely as a cloud "—that's a beautiful image, don't you think ? " Lonely as a cloud, that floats on high o'er vales and hills "—it's really a lovely poem —" When all at once I saw such a lot of daffodils——"

Miss Simpson : Rubbish, Sarah. " When all at once I saw a crowd——"

A Woman : And I wish we could see a crowd now. It's getting lonesome up here, all by ourselves.

A Woman : You bet there'd have been company at the " Traveller's Rest."

Women : Ay, there would be !

Miss Timson : Please don't mention that wretched place again . . . and if Miss Simpson can quote poetry so fluently, I suggest she recites some to you.

Women (*much alarmed*) : No, no, Miss, *please* !

A Woman : Poetry'd make us feel damper than ever.

A Woman : Must we stay here much longer, Miss ? Couldn't we be beginning the way down ?

WOMEN (*brightening visibly*) : Ay, the way down !

[*They whisper among themselves ; the words " cup o' tea " can be plainly heard.*

MISS TIMSON : No, we're *not* going down yet. I brought you here to see the view, and as I'm perfectly sure the mist is lifting at last, we'll just wait a little longer, and then you'll have the treat of your lives and be ever so grateful to me. Fancy, you'll see right as far as Bembly Bay !

A WOMAN : Who wants to see Bembly, anyway ? A one-eyed place if ever there was one !

A WOMAN : I once went out in a boat on that there bay, and——

[*Whispers. Cries of " Tut, tut " from the others.*

A WOMAN : And they do say that at some of them boarding-houses there——

[*They whisper among themselves. Cries of " Well, I never ! "*

MISS SIMPSON : They're getting out of hand, Sarah. You'd better do something.

MISS TIMSON (*asserting herself*) : Now, now, no whispering, please ! I think we'll all sing a little song to occupy our minds. Come on, now altogether—" My bonnie is over the ocean ; My bonnie is——" (*Breaks down.*) For goodness' sake, Gladys, you lead them.

MISS SIMPSON (*singing with anything but a good grace, the women attempting to follow*) : " My bonnie is over the ocean ; My bonnie is over the sea ; My bonnie——"

A WOMAN : Mist is going fair rapid now, Miss.

[*They all lean forward out of the shelter.*

MISS TIMSON (*in triumph*) : There ! What did I tell you ?

A WOMAN : There's something just over the way. (*Points to the left.*)

MISS TIMSON : It will be the buttress of a mountain. In a moment we shall see its bare, rugged flanks.

A WOMAN (*shocked*) : O-o-o, what a thing to say, Miss !

Miss Simpson : Miss Timson's only getting poetical again, Martha.

Miss Timson : Isn't it like the unfolding of a beautiful dream ? I can see the dim shapes of the everlasting hills. . . .

A Woman : More like houses, Miss.

Miss Timson : Nonsense. You're spoiling my vision.

A Woman : Houses, right enough, and oh, look there !

[*They all look to the left.*

Women : *It's the " Traveller's Rest " ! ! !*

Miss Simpson (*breaking out*) : Now, I hope you're satisfied, Sarah ! We're not at the Hospice at all. This is some wretched little shelter on the outskirts of the town ! I knew something was wrong, all the time.

Miss Timson : Nonsense, Gladys, you're always unjust to me.

[*A* Woman *steals to the left very quietly, and, with a broad smile, beckons to the others.*

I followed the map all the way most carefully.

Miss Simpson : When do you ever follow a map ? Why, when we were at Penystumllyn——

Miss Timson : Please don't bring up Penystumllyn again.

[*As they quarrel all the* Women, *on tiptoe and in high spirits, steal out behind them and hurry to the left.*

You know perfectly well there was a complete misunderstanding about a footpath.

Miss Simpson : And whose misunderstanding was it, I should like to know ? And now, to-day, just the same thing happens. You walk blindly on, too conceited to ask the way or consult a map——

Miss Timpson (*turning round*) : Didn't you all hear me ask the stationmaster—oh ! They've gone !

Miss Simpson : Where ?

Miss Timson : I can't think—oh, they're all rushing into the

40

" Traveller's Rest " ! Hi ! hi ! Mrs. Martin, Mrs. Bracegirdle, Mrs. Sugars . . . (*Runs out on the left calling wildly.*)

MISS SIMPSON (*joining in the chase*) : Hi ! hi ! Mrs. Muggleton, Mrs. Hartley, Mrs.——

[*The stage is left empty.*

Curtain.

ADULT EDUCATION

The LECTURER, *of uncertain age and still more uncertain costume, stands on the left. In front of her are two rows of chairs, with a gap in the middle suggesting the beginning of an aisle. On the chairs sit four or five women (more can be added, of course), all in rather gloomy moods. A wispy female in gym. dress lurks behind the* LECTURER. *(If the* LECTURER *and her* ASSISTANT *can be on some kind of platform, so much the better, but it is not essential.)*

LECTURER (*coming forward and smiling with winsome grace*) : Good evening. I am so delighted to see that we really have an audience. Miss Dithers, the dear warden, said she wasn't at all certain how the evening classes would be attended during this dreadful war-time, but I told her I was *sure* people would turn up, if only to show their faith in the dear old settlement and its work, and here you are. So glad ! Well, we mustn't waste time ; we must go to it, of course, he ! he ! *Well, now,* the first thing to remember about the subject on which I am privileged to address you is that the art of mime is universal. Mime, with its *vivid,* noiseless action, causes emotions similar to those experienced during a dream—so interesting, is it not ? It is really the art of suggestion, and goes far back, to Egypt, Greece, Rome, you know, all those *great* civilisations. And, in this connection, it must not be forgotten that the language of mime is universal. That does simplify matters for us all, I think, don't you ? That is, the ways of expressing emotion in the different races of mankind are identical, absolutely identical. This can be proved quite easily, and, as we cannot have practical demonstrations in a class like this too early, I will ask my assistant, Miss Donner, to step forward at once and show you what I mean. Miss Donner !

[*The wispy female sidles to the front.*

Will you give us a few primitive emotions, please !

[MISS DONNER *stretches her arms out to heaven and throws her head as far back as she can manage. The* LECTURER *turns to the audience.*

Now, tell me, what do you feel that represents ?

[*A pause. The* WOMEN *regard* MISS DONNER *apathetically, while she finds it increasingly difficult to maintain her balance.*

42

Please don't keep Miss Donner waiting. Say what you think.

A WOMAN (*slowly*) : It's what our Jimmy does when he's got a bad throat.

ANOTHER WOMAN : Ay, gargling, that's what it is.

LECTURER : Well, it's really " prayer," but we'll pass on to the next. Miss Donner !

[MISS DONNER *twists herself in corkscrew fashion, with one hand on her head and the other clasped round her middle. This time the* WOMEN *regard her with more interest.*

Now, what about that ?

A WOMAN (*slowly*) : Well, I reely wouldn't like to say what I think's the matter with 'er now, Miss.

ANOTHER WOMAN : Aw, don't be silly. It's only stomach gripes.

[MISS DONNER *relaxes quickly at this.*

LECTURER : Actually, it was " abandonment to grief," but perhaps that is what you meant. (*Whispering to* MISS DONNER) For goodness' sake, Mabel, express yourself more clearly if you can !

MISS DONNER (*hissing back*) : No use blaming your failures on me, Clara !

[*For a moment they glare at each other ; then the* LECTURER *resumes.*

LECTURER : Now, we'll have one more example, and then we *must* get on. Miss Donner !

MISS DONNER *puts one hand on her waist, extends the other hand to the audience, and, throwing her head sideways, contorts her features into a smile.*

Of course, you can guess what that is ?

A WOMAN : Saturday night.

LECTURER : Saturday night ?—keep your design, Miss Donner !—Saturday night ?

A WOMAN : I mean she's all canned up.

ANOTHER WOMAN (*explaining*) : Like some ladies do get on Saturdays, you know.

43

LECTURER : Well, it's really " friendly welcome," but perhaps we'd better get on to other matters. (*Whispering* You seem *most* unconvincing to-night, Mabel ! (*To class*) *Now*, apart from the expression of emotion, mime teaches us the value of movement. Movement should always be free, gracious, rhythmical. So one should study line and form ; it is *so* helpful, and adds quite a new interest to daily life. *Now*, take the simple, everyday action of sitting down. How often do we sit down without thinking, without making the process beautiful and rhythmic. (*Takes chair and places it in the centre.*) Miss Donner ! Will you show the class how to sit down prettily, please ?

[MISS DONNER *sits down prettily.*

There, wasn't that *nice* ? And so simple. Just five easy movements, nothing more. Now, I want you to come up in turn and try and sit on that chair just as Miss Donner did. It isn't at all difficult, really. Do come. It's such *fun* !

[*A pause ; the* WOMEN *look at each other.*

Don't be shy. Think how pleased your husbands will be when they see the ease and grace with which you do the simplest things.

A WOMAN : My husband'd turn me out if he caught me sitting down like that.

A WOMAN : Proper rude, I call it. People'd wonder what I meant.

A WOMAN : You ought to know, Miss, that after plumping ourselves down natural-like for over forty years, we're not going to bump ourselves to bits attempting impossible novelties now.

A WOMAN (*darkly*) : You could do yourself an injury, trying those games on.

WOMEN : Ay, you could an' all.

LECTURER (*depressed*) : Very well, we'd better get on to something else. (*Brightening up*) Because, quite apart from sitting down, there are so many other things we do that require a little grace adding to them. Suppose you drop a handkerchief ? We often do, don't we ? How many of you realise that there is

44

a *right* way and a *wrong* way to pick up a handkerchief? It's usually an ugly, graceless, even clumsy affair, but, in reality, it can be quite a little poem in movement. I will now drop my handkerchief, and Miss Donner will kindly pick it up. (*Drops handkerchief.*) Miss Donner!

[MISS DONNER *trips forwards, and, in a series of sweeping curves, manages to pick up the handkerchief and hand it to the* LECTURER.

Thank you. (*To class*) Wasn't that *nice*?

[*The* WOMEN *remain unconvinced.*

A WOMAN: Can't say it was, Miss.

LECTURER: Oh, but why not?

ANOTHER WOMAN: Bit too oncoming for me.

A WOMAN: Proper fast, I call it.

A WOMAN: Your young girl may be able to waggle about like that, but we haven't the figure.

A WOMAN: We'd split up the back if we tried them monkey tricks.

THE WOMEN: Ay, that's true enough.

LECTURER (*peevishly*): Well, *I* don't think you would! (*Whispering to* MISS DONNER) I must say, Mabel, you don't seem to be very successful to-night!

MISS DONNER (*snapping back*): Speak for yourself, Clara. I'm doing my best as always!

[*Again, they glare at each other for a moment.*

LECTURER (*recovering*): Oh, well, we'd better get on to something else. Now, one of the most important branches of mime is *gesture*. Of course, the fewer gestures the better, but when you make a gesture the meaning should be expressed from the arm right down to the finger-tips. It simply must *not* stop short at the wrist, leaving the hand dropping and inexpressive, like a bunch of bananas——

A WOMAN: Excuse me, Miss, but what has all this to do with plain cooking?

LECTURER: Plain cooking?

WOMAN : Yes. (*Pulls paper out of pocket.*) Syllabus says, " Six lectures on plain cooking. Room C. Tuesdays. 7.0 to 8.30. Miss Caroline Higgins. Fee 1s. 6d. for the course." That's what we've come for.

LECTURER : Plain cooking ? Room C ? Oh, dear, but this is Room D. This is a lecture on mime, gesture and deportment ! You've made a mistake.

[*The* WOMEN *rise with alacrity.*

A WOMAN (*to the others*) : I thought it was queer.

A WOMAN : Queer ? A bit disgusting, if you ask me.

A WOMAN : Her, with her sitting prettily and handkerchief flopping an' all. Come on, Matilda, we'll perhaps learn something wholesome in the next room.

A WOMAN : Ay, an' after this we'll need it !

[*Agreeing heartily, the* WOMEN *file out.*

LECTURER (*turning to her assistant*) : Mabel !

MISS DONNER : Clara !

[*They embrace for consolation.*

The fee for each and every representation of this play by amateurs is Five Shillings, payable in advance to—

MESSRS. SAMUEL FRENCH LTD.,
26 SOUTHAMPTON STREET,
STRAND, LONDON, W.C.2

or their authorised agents, who, upon payment of the fee, will issue a licence for the performance to take place.

No performance may be given unless this licence has been obtained.

EARLY PIT

Six WOMEN (*more can be added if desired*) *stand, informally, two by two in a row, with* MISS MARGARET *by herself at the end. They are waiting for the early pit door of a theatre to open. There is no need for this door to be shown, although some kind of a door on the left with " Early Pit " marked above it would be helpful. The* WOMEN *are of all types, and are evidently dressed for an outing.* MISS MARGARET, *in charge of the group, is a good-natured, fussy Vicar's daughter of indeterminate age.*

1ST WOMAN (*nearest to the door*) : Well, I must say, Miss Margaret, it's wonderful how you found your way to the theatre without asking anybody at all.

MISS MARGARET : Oh, I'm quite used to this town, you know. After all, my dear father, the Vicar, was once a curate here— (*hastily*)—not that I remember anything about that, of course.

3RD WOMAN (*wonderingly*) : Why ever not, Miss ?

2ND WOMAN (*tactfully interposing*) : Now, Hannah !—Anyway, the place will have changed a bit since then.

MISS MARGARET : Yes, indeed ; they're always enlarging and altering things. But still, as you admit, I've brought you to the early pit door without mishap !

4TH WOMAN : You did, for sure, Miss Margaret. You must have one of them bumps of locality.

6TH WOMAN : Well, it doesn't look as if Annie'd got one, does it ?

5TH WOMAN : You may well say that. Why, she ought to have been here ages ago. But then, that girl's only half-baked, although it's her own auntie as says so.

1ST WOMAN : Was she always a bit knocked like, Mrs. Staggs ?

5TH WOMAN : Always. Even as a child she was for ever saying queer things and looking peculiar.

3RD WOMAN (*sympathetically*) : Ah, it's bad when they're like that.

MISS MARGARET : Now, you really must not say unkind things about dear Annie. She has many good points. And if she

47

dislikes trains and prefers to come by bus, she has a perfect right to do so, hasn't she?

5TH WOMAN : That's all very well, Miss Margaret, but in the family we call that kind of thing our Annie's awkwardness. Why shouldn't she come with us others? What's the idea of coming by herself, grand like, on a bus?

2ND WOMAN : Ay; ain't we good enough for her, or what?

4TH WOMAN : And where's her awkwardness led her to, anyway? She's not here. (*Lowering her voice*) Anything can happen in a town of this size.

6TH WOMAN : You're right there. Some of those chaps——

[*Much whispering.*

MISS MARGARET : Oh, come; we mustn't be gloomy. Probably the bus is late.

1ST WOMAN : I don't hold with buses myself. They go that fast your inside's upset before you know where you are.

2ND WOMAN : Ay. You remember that bout I had when we were going to Windermere? I always blamed bus for that.

6TH WOMAN : It was more pork-pies than bus, Mrs. Slater.

MISS MARGARET : Now, we really must forget all unfortunate happenings in the past. Remember, we're out to enjoy ourselves.

3RD WOMAN : That's right, Miss Margaret. As I always say, enjoy yourself, even if you are married.

5TH WOMAN : And if our Annie misses the show, it's her own fault.

2ND WOMAN : Ay, that's the right way to look at it.

6TH WOMAN : Speaking for myself, I hope she does miss it. It'll teach her not to be so uppish.

MISS MARGARET : Now, we just must *not* be uncharitable. . . . Let me see, do any of you know anything about the play this afternoon? All I know is that you asked me to be sure to choose an amusing one.

1ST WOMAN : That's what we want, Miss Margaret. Something to cheer us up. And they tell me this piece is proper funny.

4TH WOMAN : A roar from start to finish. That's what paper said.

MISS MARGARET : Well, I most sincerely hope it comes up to your expectations. Personally, I should have preferred something a little more serious. . . .

3RD WOMAN : Now, you know, Miss Margaret, after the experience of last year, you promised that kind of thing shouldn't happen again.

2ND WOMAN : I wasn't at the out last year with my sister being took bad. What happened ?

SEVERAL WOMEN : Oh, it was awful !

1ST WOMAN (*to* 2ND WOMAN) : You know, it was called " Murder in the Cathedral," and we were up a gum-tree from start to finish. I'm sure I don't know what it was all about, except that a man who said he was Thomas Becket——

MISS MARGARET : Now, my dears, we simply will not talk about last year. You must remember that my dear Father especially wanted you to see the play, and I wish you would believe me when I say that it is one of the most wonderful——

4TH WOMAN : It may have been wonderful, Miss Margaret, but I haven't got over it yet. First, there was buckets full of poetry, and then they killed the old man, and then——

6TH WOMAN : I quite agree with you, Mrs. Slatters ; it was a bit thick. Still, all the time I kept saying to myself, thank God it isn't Shakespeare.

MISS MARGARET (*shocked*) : Now, Mrs. March, that really is a little too bad of you ! Shakespeare is our national poet ?

5TH WOMAN : Well, Miss Margaret, he may be, but, personally, he always gives me the 'orrors.

MISS MARGARET : But, Mrs. Staggs, the comedies——!

5TH WOMAN : Well, you wouldn't call them really *funny*, would you ? I mean, one laughs a bit out of politeness, but all the time you've a sinking feeling inside——

3RD WOMAN (*changing the subject*) : Anyway, Minnie, we ain't

49

going to get no sinking feeling this afternoon. Why, look at the title—" Spot the Spotter ! " That's a good beginning, isn't it ?

Miss MARGARET : I'm afraid I think it's a vulgar title, and will probably be a vulgar play, and I haven't dared to tell dear Father much about it. But as you all subscribed to this outing, it seemed only fair to let you have your own choice this year.

2ND WOMAN (*softly*) : And about time, too.

1ST WOMAN (*also softly*) : You hush, Martha. You know Miss Margaret intends well, whatever she may do.

2ND WOMAN : And you know 'ell's completely paved with——

1ST WOMAN : You hush, I tell you. You can't talk about 'ell here. (*Louder.*) They say, Miss Margaret, that this is one of them comic crime pieces, and the detective's a fair knock-out. My cousin Mary says she split her sides when she went last Monday. It's been such a success it's retained for a fortnight.

4TH WOMAN : Then it's surprising there are not more people waiting, isn't it ?

6TH WOMAN : Seems as if we're the only ones.

3RD WOMAN : I expect it's only their stingy natures. You bet they're all outside the ordinary pit, too miserly to pay the extra.

5TH WOMAN : Ay, that'll be it. Barnsfold people always were as mean as mean. My old grandfather always said the meanest creature he ever met came from Barnsfold—and yet, he married her, poor fool !

1ST WOMAN : Still, if we'd known, we might just as well waited outside ordinary pit and saved our money.

2ND WOMAN : Suppose we try that door now ?

[*General movement towards the left.*

Miss MARGARET (*holding up a hand*) : Oh, my dears, I don't advise it. If it's as you say, there may be ever so many people by now round the corner and we should only get bad seats ; or worse, not get in at all.

5TH WOMAN : There's a good bit in what Miss Margaret says,

50

especially as it's nearly time this door opened. If only our Annie—— (*Looks towards the right.*)

2ND WOMAN : If she arrives late, will she have the nous to come straight in, do you think ?

6TH WOMAN : Not her. You bet she don't know the meaning of the word nous.

MISS MARGARET (*brightly*) : Well, do you know, I'm never quite sure I do. Won't you explain ?

6TH WOMAN (*hurriedly*) : You see, Miss Margaret, if you was eating an apple and I was to say " Hi ! " (*hitting* MISS MARGARET) " there's a scorpion inside——"

MISS MARGARET (*startled*) : Oh, how dreadful !

6TH WOMAN : You wouldn't eat the apple, would you ? Well, that'd be nous.

MISS MARGARET (*confused*) : I know I'm awfully stupid, but I still——

1ST WOMAN : They're coming ! I can hear 'em opening the doors !

[*Noise of bolts being withdrawn. General excitement.*

2ND WOMAN : Get your money ready, girls, we'll soon be in now !

1ST WOMAN (*as door opens*) : Hurray ! (*To* 2ND WOMAN) Come on, Martha.

2ND WOMAN (*as she follows* 1ST WOMAN *in*) : I never felt more ready for a laugh in my life. What with my stomach and Jimmy's chicken-pox——

[*Exit with* 1ST WOMAN.

3RD WOMAN (*going in with* 4TH WOMAN) : I must remember the jokes to tell our Alf. He's only three, but he's that quick——

4TH WOMAN : My old man doesn't hold with jokes at all, so I wait till he's gone out and then——

[*They exit.*

6TH WOMAN (*to* 5TH WOMAN) : Now, Minnie, get a move on.

5TH WOMAN : I think I'll stop here a moment to see if our Annie comes. Miss Margaret, you go in with Eliza.

MISS MARGARET : Thank you, Mrs. Staggs. It's very sweet of you to be so solicitous for your niece—and we'll be sure to keep a good place for you inside.

[*She exits with* 6TH WOMAN. *At which moment* ANNIE *appears on the right, out of breath.*

ANNIE : O-o-o, Auntie ! Hurry up and come along, or there won't be a seat left !

5TH WOMAN : What do you mean, you silly girl ? There are plenty of seats left. Where have you been all this time ?

ANNIE : Waiting for you all outside the Palace.

5TH WOMAN : You great soft thing, this is the Palace, where " Spot the Spotter " 's on.

ANNIE : Oh, no, this is the Royal.

5TH WOMAN : Are you *sure* ? (ANNIE *nods vigorously.*) Then what's on here ?

ANNIE : The bills outside say " Hamlet."

5TH WOMAN : Gosh ! Is the Palace far away ?

ANNIE : Only 'bout three minutes, but do hurry. The crowd's terrific.

5TH WOMAN : Right ho, Annie. We'll run for it !

[*They run out on the left.*

52

CINDERELLA

A Potted Panto

CHARACTERS

FAIRY QUEEN.
DEMON KING.
CINDERELLA
THE UGLY SISTERS.
PRINCE.
HERALD.
MOB.

NOTE.—*Each scene ends with a brief black out.*

SCENE I

FAIRY QUEEN : I've a particular interest in Cinderella.
And would like her married to some good fella.

DEMON KING : I'll bring your scheme to naught, I vow,
And she'll never get further than where she is now.

FAIRY QUEEN : As to that, we'll wait and see.
The last laugh is the best, he ! he !

[*They strike at each other with their wands and exit, the* FAIRY
QUEEN *left, looking upwards with a beatific smile ; the* DEMON
KING *right, snarling and scowling.*

SCENE II

CINDERELLA (*musing*) : Here live I among the cinders.
Scrubbing floors and cleaning winders.
Not allowed a single day out :
How I wish there were a way out !

1ST UGLY SISTER : While we're at the ball to-night
Mind you keep the fire alight.

2ND UGLY SISTER : When we return, no longer frisky,
We shall need some nice hot whisky !

[*Exit, giggling and slapping each other.*

53

CINDERELLA (*alone and depressed*) : They've gone, the hags, all rouge and paste.
An ensemble in the worst of taste !

[*She weeps.*

DEMON KING (*appearing and sneering*) : While you, you fool, must do your duty,
Slutting at home, despite your beauty.

[*Exit with a cruel laugh.*

FAIRY QUEEN (*appearing, all smiles*) : Nay, never heed him, dearest child.
Your fairy godmother, sweet and mild,
Has come with pumpkin, mice and all,
To send you revelling to the ball.

CINDERELLA : If you're hinting at that coach-and-four trick,
It's out of date ; we're now much more slick.
Obtain, if you're so very clever,
A car, the most expensive ever.

[FAIRY QUEEN *waves wand ; noise of car outside.*

SCENE III

FAIRY QUEEN : You've got your dress, you've got your car,
So all the best, my dear, ta, ta.

CINDERELLA : I don't complain, but these glass slippers
Hurt like a ruddy lobster's nippers.*

FAIRY QUEEN : You've got to follow some of the story,
And don't forget, at twelve your glory
Will go as though't had never been ;
So come back here before you're seen.

SCENE IV

PRINCE (*to the* UGLY SISTERS) : Good gad, my dears, who is that maiden ?

1ST UGLY SISTER : Some gate-crasher with cheek o'erladen.

PRINCE : She's ravishing ! To dance I'll ask her.

* *Alternative line :* Are like a pair of lobster's nippers.

54

2ND UGLY SISTER : He's gone !

1ST UGLY SISTER :   Good Lord !

BOTH :   This is disaster !

[*They faint in each other's arms.*

SCENE V

PRINCE (*dancing with* CINDERELLA) : Your name, my sweetest,
    tell me truly.

CINDERELLA : Your curiosity's unruly.
Just take me as I am, your Highness.

PRINCE (*chucking her under the chin*) : How I adore your modest
    shyness.

[*Cuckoo clock begins.*

CINDERELLA : Oh, hang ! I now must vanish quite,
Just when the party's getting bright.

[*Runs out.*

PRINCE : She's gone. Can no one try to trip her ?
And look, by Jove, she's left her slipper !

SCENE VI

CINDERELLA (*entering, limping, without slipper*) : Well, that was
    a do and no mistake——
But the Prince's S.A.'s simply great.

DEMON KING (*appearing and sneering*) : You've only been an
    interloper,
And left your slipper—that's a *faux pas* !

[*Vanishes with a cruel laugh.*

HERALD (*entering*) : By order of the Prince I'm here.
Behold this slipper, crystal clear.
If any maid can fit it on,
The Prince will marry her anon.

1ST UGLY SISTER : Now's our chance—but goodness gracious

2ND UGLY SISTER : Our feet, I fear, are far too spacious.

CINDERELLA : Damnation take these shoes again,*
But the Prince is worth a little pain.
(*Fits on slipper.*) Ah ha, my dears, now pray observe,
I gain the prize which I deserve.

[*Enter the* PRINCE, *followed by the mob.*

PRINCE : Kindly announce both far and wide,
That Cinderella is my bride.

[*Grand flourish of trumpets.*

DEMON KING (*appearing*) : Permit me to forbid the banns :
The story's old and full of shams.

FAIRY QUEEN (*appearing*) : The time for criticism's gone by
now ;
You're nothing but a blasted highbrow !

[*Strikes him with her wand ; he falls. She stands with one foot on him and addresses the mob.*

Let all give way to joy and laughter ;
The couple'll be happy ever after !

The CURTAIN *falls to universal rejoicing.*

* *Alternative line :* I hate to wear these things again.

The fee for each and every representation of this play by amateurs is Five Shillings, payable in advance to—

MESSRS. SAMUEL FRENCH LTD.,
26 SOUTHAMPTON STREET,
STRAND, LONDON, W.C.2

or their authorised agents, who, upon payment of the fee, will issue a licence for the performance to take place.

No performance may be given unless this licence has been obtained.